Steps to
Health, W
& Inner Peace

Francis ☺'Neill

A *Making Sense of It* **book**

Steps to Health, Wealth & Inner Peace

A *Making Sense of It* book

ISBN: 978-0-9934626-6-5 (Paperback)

May 2019. Launch of paperback version with new cover. Previously in eBook only. Includes minor revision of content; updating the August 2018 revision of the eBook version, and adding a new book cover.

This book includes an Index

Editor: Annie Locke

Printed by: Kindle Direct Publishing

Cover: Image of vector tree and arrows, by **topor**, included in design.

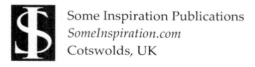
Some Inspiration Publications
SomeInspiration.com
Cotswolds, UK

Contents

A true companion of **Steps to Health, Wealth & Inner Peace**

Introduction

This book has been a real joy to write, particularly as I have been thinking, experiencing and writing around the topics covered here for some years, and now have a chance to share them with you.

"Steps..." is intended as a handy and practical reference book for dealing with some of life's essentials. It began as an *aide-memoire* to myself – sparked by articles I'd written – to remind me of what is important going forward. And it might surprise you: I do read back through it quite often for those reminders. I'm one of life's learners let's say.

It is a reminder of the simple steps one can take – indeed steps one really ought to take – in order so as to keep life and soul together, to be true to oneself and successful in one's endeavours.

Comment on the steps

You don't have a soul. You are a soul. You have a body.

C S Lewis

Like C S Lewis, from my perspective too we are each a spirit or soul having a physical body.

Our body is a beautiful piece of kit that, given it is fully-functioning (as not everyone is blessed with all parts working to their optimum potential), it is well designed for existing on our planet – it is our Earthsuit. And if looked after properly, fed, watered, rested and kept in good shape, it will last for years.

In order to achieve and maintain good health though we also need to have a healthy and wholesome mind, and be working with our spirit. This way, I believe, lies the path to a well-adjusted successful and happy life.

Nourish and balance your mind, body and spirit, and you won't go far wrong in life. The following steps invite you to do just that. If you are in need, and apply all of the steps in this book, it will seriously help you to change your life for the better. Rest assured this is a "given," if you apply what you learn.

Begin here then to get your life into gear – using some simple measures for some extremely positive outcomes.

Mind

Simple Steps to help get your mind into gear

You were born with wings, why prefer to crawl through life?
Jalāl ad-Dīn Muhammad Rūmī

The only person you are destined to become is the person you decide to be.
Ralph Waldo Emerson

This section will provide you with some useful tools, and food, for creative thought in more ways than one...

Seven Principles Leading to Success

I want to begin this section not with steps as such but with some important principles I've learned about, from a number of years ago.

Back in the 1980s I did a piece of research that involved ten successful entrepreneurs and business owners (i.e. running their respective businesses at a profit for five years or more). Four of them were millionaires.

This was part of a study looking into what business people considered was their "recipe for success" – what they thought were the guiding principles behind their successes.

The outcome was honed down to the following seven principles that they all could agree upon in running their businesses successfully. Here they are:

1. Get out of the "blame game"
2. Know who you are – what gives your life "meaning"
3. Plan ahead – have a business or project plan
4. Be prepared to step out of your comfort zone
5. Become an authority
6. Make "giving up" not an option – be in it for the long game
7. Keep your eye on the ball

I'm thinking these are as valid today as ever – and important to share with you here. In terms of working with, these principles don't necessarily have to follow in that order, but there is a natural sequence to it.

I'm seeing these as good foundation stones upon which to build all the steps that follow in this book.

The suggestion is that, if you want to become successful with your life then consider applying these principles. While the survey was linked to developing a project or business enterprise, in essence these principles can be just as easily applied to having a successful approach to fulfilling your life, your dreams, your goals and ambitions, in most any direction.

1. Get out of the "blame game"

You've no doubt heard the saying, "A bad workman blames his own tools." On one level of course this literally refers to the tools the workman (or workwoman) is using, but in other respects the "tools" being blamed could be a host of things.

It could be people, such as our friends, our partners, our family, the people who live next door, or our work colleagues that are to blame for things not going right, for the situation we find ourselves in. It could be the company we work for. It could extend out to our government. It could be not having enough time in the day. It could be the traffic, or the weather that's to blame...

It is perhaps easier to blame our lot on anything and everything, "out there" in the external world, rather than take responsibility for our own situation "in here."

You, and I, will have to look behind our external world and possibly dig deep to understand that we are ever attracting circumstances towards us, consciously or subconsciously by our beliefs and attitude to life.

Keep this in mind as you read through the topics on self-hypnosis and creative visualisation below. This book will certainly provide you with more than clues to this attraction, and importantly, ways of changing or handling it.

2. Know who you are – what gives your life "meaning"

And so to the second principle they could agree upon. This reminded me of the inscription over the Temple of Apollo at Delphi, in ancient Greece, that is the words, *"Know Thyself"* (γνῶθι σεαυτὸν).

Temple of Apollo Delphi Photo: Paul Caputo

To know who one truly is and to live by that knowledge is the obvious interpretation.

The survey outcome was also more practical, taking it to mean knowing your abilities, learning needs and also knowing your limitations.

Also knowing what you want from life and being prepared to follow your own star – to have belief in yourself, in what gives your life meaning.

This can be challenging for many of us to know what we actually want from life. It can take time to reflect on the matter.

We are encouraged to make such choices, usually around our career, quite early on in our lives. And, before we know where we are, we have become wedded to our circumstances, our way of living that, when we reflect upon it, may not be so agreeable or suitable, or what we truly wanted from life.

And the argument follows to not let ourselves be led away from our goals by other people who think they know what is in our best interests. And while, by all means, we need to give attention to criticism that is constructive, we don't willy-nilly leave ourself open to negative criticism, particularly when we are starting out.

In context it was also suggested that it is usually a good idea to keep your goals, your dreams, under wraps until you have developed them into a structure that has practical working application or outcomes – that you have confidence in. Then share and listen to objective feedback if you want to. Objective and constructive feedback needs to be welcomed, a necessity in making progress.

3. Plan ahead – have a business or project plan

Have a plan of action for your project or enterprise. Don't for a minute think it will all fall into place by itself – it won't!

Have a plan of action for where you want to be in a given period of time. Include what you need to resource your project, and any training you will need to meet your objectives. Planning and accounting (see 5. below) allows you control over your direction, and affords you the opportunity to gauge your route to success. It also helps you to maintain momentum.

4. Be prepared to step out of your comfort zone

> *Failures do what is tension relieving, while winners do what is goal achieving.*
>
> Denis Waitley

What often separates successful people from the unsuccessful is that they believe passionately in what they are doing.

It would seem that most of us are happy to go through the week, indeed for some our whole lives, with as little stress, and as few problems, as possible.

When you choose to live your life with direction and purpose, your main concern is succeeding with your objectives, your goals. It probably won't be an easy path.

This may well call on you to go that extra mile, putting in those extra hours, leaving behind safe 9 to 5 routines, missing out on that "night out," having a work/home life out of balance, taking on challenges, doing things you never thought you would have to do, or be capable of doing.

5. Become an authority

Aim to become the expert, an authority in your field of interest. Become disciplined, thorough and punctual.

Keep a check on your activities, projections and spending – keep a log, keep accounts, list your incomings and outgoings.

If you want to be successful you need to take what you offer seriously, and be professional about it. Develop a strong work ethic and strive to be the best at what you do. Do everything you need to do to improve. Get the skills you need. Organise your time and use it wisely towards success.

Check out the competition in your field and endeavour to be better, the best.

What was also voiced here is that becoming an authority does not mean being overly self-sufficient or controlling.

No one is an island. You are most probably going to need help. Be ever-ready to delegate to others who are better placed to help you towards meeting your commitments and achieving your goals.

6. Make "giving up" not an option – be in it for the long game

This came up as a prominent suggestion in the survey. You must be fully committed to your project, your enterprise.

Given that you are realistic and happy that your plan is achievable; given that you are passionate about your goals and are ready to take that step to initiate your progress towards them. Given that you are ready to begin, then make the commitment, and make "giving-up" a no-no as part of your credo.

Giving up is not necessarily the same as failing at something you have put your heart and soul into. Even then, when it looks like "the end is nigh," there may be another way into achieving your goals.

Think on this; winners will tend to put their failures down to an opportunity for "learning from mistakes," with the aim to get it right next time.

Psychologically you can get past "tried but didn't succeed with that approach" easier than "I gave up" on a goal or dream. The latter can do something to one's psyche.

Having set a precedent, it can certainly make the next project or enterprise, or step, that much harder and less likely to succeed. And what's more you may have fewer supporters rooting for you.

7. Keep your eye on the ball

Keep your eye on the ball. In other words, stay focussed on your goals, and avoid becoming distracted.

Usually a lot of enthusiasm and energy goes into initiating a new plan of action. But, once underway, it can become attractive to relax in one's efforts – perhaps even more so when facing early setbacks and knocks at the coal face.

The advice is to stay focussed with your dreams and not fritter energy on non-essential matters.

Almost certainly what you plan will contain challenges and opportunity to lose focus. You'll find many success stories out there that didn't win on an easy ride.

Final comment – Be ready!

A general consensus stressed the importance of timing and taking that leap of faith. If you are ready to pursue your dream, your enterprise, then do it now!

Don't procrastinate or over-plan for all eventualities. Don't deliberate for too long! Remember time and tide waits for no one – and how quickly opportunity can slip by...

Results

Results will depend on applying these principles in context with your goals. With everything pointing in the right direction these are principles you can adapt towards having an authentic and successful life.

A book I'd recommend you read in this context is, Stephen Covey's, *The 7 Habits of Highly Effective People*. Covey's "habits" (a different set from the seven above) endorse the principles here but gives greater focus to living with fairness, integrity, honesty and dignity. It is more than worth a read...

Steps to Improving Your Subconscious Mind

It is a wonderful thing to incorporate healthy guiding principles (as discussed above) into our life. To stick by them however may be a different story; requiring change at a deeper level.

This is especially so when our past has taught us to live by a different set of principles or rules – not necessarily quite so in-keeping, healthy, passionate or optimistic.

So here we are going to explore how, if need be, we may change our habitual state of mind into something better.

Let me begin by asking how you are

Are you:
- o Lacking in confidence?
- o In need of relaxing more?
- o Anxious?
- o Having difficulty sleeping?
- o Trying to lose weight?
- o Inclined to procrastinate?
- o In need of bringing more joy into your life?
- o Desiring to be more adept at learning?
- o Concerned with wanting to improve your memory?
- o Wanting to bring more money into your life?
- o Desiring to improve your relationships?

If you can answer "Yes" to any of these questions, and probably more besides (had I listed them), then let me suggest you can start to resolve your issues by taking action today.

Help yourself

What do I mean by "taking action?" A simple tried and regularly tested way to go about improving your life is through hypnosis, or by use of subliminal persuasion! The methods, and the belief that it works, have been around for years.

How it works

Put simply, what you think and habitually believe about yourself and your world is actually dynamic.

Your thoughts and beliefs influence your actions, intentions, directions, and what you then draw towards you.

Consider this: *Your inner life creates your outer life.*

This is true whether driven by your subconscious mind or what you consciously want or don't want to happen in your life. It is important to be aware of this, particularly the latter part.

Most of us are likely to think that this works the other way around – the external world influencing what we think, believe and act on.

We know full well we are continually bombarded by all kinds of stimulus and messages by our interaction with our world. To some extent this can influence, sometimes profoundly so, what we think, believe and act on, but to a greater extent our current take on our world is driven by an

---

older strata of our experience. This is at a level below what we call the conscious mind. In other words it is the subconscious mind.

Your subconscious holds years of experience and learning, whether these are good or painful experiences, from childhood onwards.

It is this learning, and those experiences, from way back, that gave form to, and later developed into, patterns of behaviour and beliefs. The view is that our history of experience, particularly up to when we were six or seven years old, colours our present thoughts and perceptions about ourself and our world.

Your subconscious works on the basis of what has worked for you in the past is tried and tested, and best policy, the path of least resistance, is to stick to it now whether it is supporting your success in life or actually holding you back from the success you seek.

So how does this work?

Say, for instance, as a child, your parents were very protective of you, always concerned about your safety. They didn't like you riding your bike because you were likely to hurt yourself, they didn't like you playing with other children, in case you hurt yourself.

Unless you were very strong to ignore their advice, you likely grew up avoiding things that may hurt you; and then find, later in life, it difficult to take risks. After all, your subconscious might say, "You have succeeded in life thus far without big risks, so let's keep it this way."

There is always the possibility, of course, of your going the other way in reaction to your background. This might mean that you are now inclined to take rash and dangerous risks, in attempts to break away from the influence of the past. Either way may not be healthy. It comes to represent your instinctual approach to life.

Let's consider a person who grew up in a family of modest means where affection or encouragement was rarely expressed or demonstrated. Such families do exist. The likelihood is that this person will grow up lacking in self-confidence, having low self-esteem and expectations of their life.

The likelihood is that, coming from the back of the grid, they will find it difficult to believe that they can create the life they want, or get away from their past. It probably won't even occur to them.

A strong individual may break through such a tough upbringing – and be stronger for it – but still with baggage.

You need your subconscious

Let me be clear here that there is nothing wrong with what we are calling the "subconscious mind." There is nothing wrong with the way that it works. It responds, reacts according to how it has been taught to respond and react – from what has gone before. It is as simple as that.

If you think about it, we live a large chunk of our lives on auto-pilot, or in other words, instinctually. We don't need to think consciously about the need to breathe, or to walk, or to talk. Lessons we have learned in the past we build into perceptions, routines, habits, and we regularly put our learning into practice without thinking too much about it.

Our ability to learn and absorb that learning frees us up to get on with other things. It can also be important to our survival as we need to be able to respond quickly, habitually, to a great many events taking place around us. That would be impossible if we had to examine and evaluate every situation or event as it arose, as though each was new to us, each time it happened.

Imagine for instance if each time you got into your car it was like the first time you had ever driven. Each time you would have to relearn the routine of driving – and be aware of all the accompanying dangers as if they were new too.

Driving a car is a good example of how we develop a habit whereby we can free up our conscious attention to focus elsewhere. In this case our conscious attention being focussed less on the act of driving the car and rather on the direction we are taking it, what's happening in front of us and around us – and perhaps the conversation we are having with our passenger/s.

Powerful patterns but not insurmountable

Probably most, but not all of our learning and habits, are necessarily healthy. Imagine, for example, if, instead of cautious parents (as in the example above), we had very ambitious parents and we learnt through our childhood that we were meant to succeed, and not supposed to fail or make mistakes at anything we do. And let's say that if we do fail, bad things could happen to us. You can probably guess what our instinctual reaction to challenges later in life might be – if we were to continue this learning through.

I suspect we will either tend towards winning at all costs, or, on the other hand, we will tend to avoid putting ourselves in a position where we could fail or make mistakes. We might be more inclined to cheat, or bend the rules, in order to secure a win. Or we might be inclined to always *play safe* and only rarely ever take a risk – that is, when it is pretty safe to do so.

Although such a habit can be well and truly entrenched, and now forms part of our identity, it will be a challenge but not impossible to transform. In order to bring about, let's say, a healthier, more positive dialogue with our world – with real consequences – we need to "change the record" so to speak.

In simple terms, in our examples, we may need to take on a new narrative around *self-acceptance, building confidence* and overcoming a *lack of love*, a *fear of failure, or fear of getting hurt* (wherein it is okay to make mistakes if we take risks, it is okay to seek encouragement and reward) until the new narrative is habitual and replaces the old record. Until, like driving the car, we do it naturally, on auto-pilot.

From the hypnotherapy perspective, one can achieve this by using hypnosis (open suggestions encouraging a state of self-induced hypnosis) and, or by subliminal persuasion (hidden suggestions, often placed in music, and given to the subconscious). These techniques have been shown to be powerful and really work – especially when they are applied with the right amount of repetition.

By changing your mind at this level you change your outlook and what you draw towards you – healthier and more positive conditions.

If this interests you, check out the following self-hypnosis methods and steps to creating positive change. I'm going to begin with a version of *The Betty Erickson Self-hypnosis Method*. You'll find variations of this method on the Web. The following is a full version.

The Betty Erickson Self-hypnosis Method

Here's what we can call a genuine self-hypnosis method – as it relies on you doing it entirely for yourself.

I'll just mention that Betty was the wife of Milton Erickson (who is often considered the most influential hypnotist of all time). She describes a method for inducing self-hypnosis as follows:

Eyes open steps

1. Find a comfortable place so that you can sit and relax – with feet flat on the floor. Let your body relax. Run a check on each part of your body that it is relaxed.
2. Breathe slowly and focus your attention in front of you – at about normal eye level.
3. Decide, and tell yourself, how long you want to practice this hypnosis for – perhaps 10 to 15 minutes.

    This helps your subconscious to become aware of the time limit, and to give you a nudge when the time has elapsed.
4. Next decide what you would like to achieve with the hypnosis session. This is an opportunity to tell your subconscious that you want to change something.

    Make it something to improve your life, what you perceive as a block or obstacle to your progress or success.

    You can just decide it, and say it to yourself. Alternatively write it down as statement of the result/s you want from the hypnosis.

    Doing the latter can help you give form to what you want, help you to clarify, and refer to, what you are seeking to alter or to understand.

5. When ready you next focus on what you can see, hear and feel.

   To begin with; focus on three things in front of you. Give each item some time and say what they are to yourself as you do so.

   These can be small things like a small part of the pattern on some wallpaper, or a shadow, or a mark on a wall or door will do.
6. Next focus on what you can hear. Separate out three sounds that you pick up on around you. Say to yourself what each sound is as you do so.
7. Next focus on three things that you can feel. Feel each of them for a reasonable amount of time.

   Subtle feelings count here – like a shoe leaning on your foot (actually it is best not to be wearing shoes for the session), or maybe an itch, or a bit of tension somewhere in your body, or the higher or lower temperature in a part of your body.
8. This completes that round.

   What you do now is repeat the process of focusing on things you see, hear and feel but only for two things each. Then, when you have completed this, you do it again, but with only one thing each time. The repetition is important because it helps you to convince your subconscious mind that you really mean to make something happen.

Next the eyes closed steps

Now again you focus on what you see, hear and feel but this time with your eyes closed and focused internally – and you repeat the procedure of three, then two then one.

1. Shut your eyes. Bring to mind an image.

   Make it an easy image to imagine. You want everything in this process to be gentle and relaxing. Be accepting of whatever image comes to your mind.

   Now bring to mind a second image, and then a third. If you have difficulty calling up an image try focussing on something that you like. Name the images as you do so.
2. Next, allow your mind to hear three sounds and name each. Accept whatever comes to you.

These could be objective sounds, external or internal, or subjective sounds, ones that you are visualising – such as the sound of lapping waves as you walk along a seashore.

3. Do the same with registering feelings – and name each.

They could be sensory experiences, such as feeling the heat from the Sun on the seashore, or they could be moods or emotion you feel. Use visualization to do this and accept whatever you feel.

4. Continue now, calling up two images, two sounds and two feelings, then going on to one of each.

When you are finished, or your subconscious gives you a nudge, open your eyes. Take stock of where you are. Take a few deep breaths and have a stretch if you need to.

You may find at this point that you feel relaxed and at peace, but, depending on what you were seeking to achieve from the self-hypnosis, you may now importantly feel something has become clearer, or has shifted even slightly.

You'll need to go through the process much more than once to establish a new pattern of belief and or behaviour – and you will get better at it with practice.

Using hypnosis programs

Rather than taking yourself through the Betty Erickson Method on a regular basis – or conceivably writing your own script, recording it and playing it back to yourself on a regular basis, as an alternative – it makes a lot of sense (and requires a lot less effort) to use a ready-made program.

In other words, you turn to an expert in the field of hypnosis to facilitate and provide you with a session tailored for your "self-hypnosis" needs. Check out the following steps:

Step 1. Get the right program

If pursuing this approach appeals to you, you'll find there are a number of online companies and practitioners on the market offering products and services to help you with whatever you are attempting to resolve. Shop around on the Web for downloads.

You might for example begin with exploring the products from Hypnosis Downloads,[1] an excellent UK company, to get a sense of what is available. This is a company I use. I've also used Potentials Unlimited in the past. You'll find companies, like these, offer a large range of hypnosis products.

Step 2. Using the program

In a way it helps to compare this with taking a course of medicine, but for the mind. The program you get will probably require you to spend around 15 to 40 minutes or so of your time each day to listen to it, but the dosage should be clear from the MP3 (or video) you receive.

If you have access to both self-hypnosis and subliminal persuasion versions, then you may find it appropriate to use the self-hypnosis at a quiet time, when you won't be disturbed, and the subliminal version during other times in your day.

The subliminal version can usually (but do always check product advice first) be listened to any time during the day, while you are getting on with your daily activities, such as driving to work, using a computer (which is how/when I use it), or during any number of activities you can do while wearing headphones.

With the self-hypnosis version you will ideally need a quiet space and allocate some time to it. Advice varies, depending on the provider and the issue you are working on, but often it is advised to use before going to bed.

Whether heading to bed or not, you'll probably find it most comfortable to sit in an easy chair or lie down – and let it waft over you. If you nod off, during the session, that's okay and often an anticipated outcome.

Step 3. How long to use for results

One might ask, how long is a piece of string. There will probably be guidelines with the program you purchase. In my experience it is not a bad idea to work on for 30 days before stopping.

I would suggest that at 30 days you take a break, move onto another program, if you have one, or return to the same program after a short break – say a week later. But, after having said that, I would encourage you to be guided by your needs, and the progress you are making.

Results

You can expect results to begin to happen during or after the period of time you are meant to use the program.

I have experienced changes almost immediately. Some of which might occasionally be down to a placebo effect, but if so it has happened on a regular basis. What you need to know is that it is helping long term – and that will only be discovered over time.

Hypnosis is subjective by nature but with tangible outcomes. It will vary from person to person, and according to how well you have stuck with the program. It will also depend on what you are seeking to achieve, and how big a mountain you are aiming at. You may notice feelings of wellbeing becoming a regular experience, at very least.

If your concern was, say, one of building confidence, has your confidence improved? If relaxation; are you able to relax more? If a sleep issue; are you sleeping better? Is your memory improving? Have you got more money coming into your life? Have you stopped smoking? Are you taking off those pounds and keeping them off?

What I will say is that it is really important that you get with the concept that **you are resetting your mind for success**, in the direction you are going. Give yourself every opportunity for this to happen.

I'd also suggest you look for change taking place around you, in what you are drawing towards you, in circumstances, events, new situations, perhaps in your old contacts, perhaps new contacts coming into your life and others departing. Again this will depend upon what you are seeking to resolve.

A comment on affirmations

I've left "affirmations" (repeating affirming words or statements to oneself towards encouraging positive outcomes) essentially to one side within the scope of this book. This is mostly for reason that, while not the same, they are, nevertheless, closely akin to the intentions of hypnosis, and the use of creative visualisation.

Some people find affirmations really powerful. Here are couple of affirmations that I really like; that you can say throughout your day, and they do help:

I am whole, perfect, strong, powerful, loving, harmonious and happy.

Charles F Haanel

Money is good. I love people and I use money. Money is a servant; I am the master.

Bob Proctor

That said, I'm inclined to the view that they work best in support of hypnosis and visualisations. I'm not so sure they are that powerful by themselves.

This is because when you are saying an affirmation to yourself you are not necessarily getting past your conscious mind to your subconscious, and so the effect can be much reduced, to the point of being cancelled out.

Also affirmations require you repeat them at regular intervals during the day – which requires effort and the tendency to slip into a routine of simply saying words that have lost their efficacy. But read on for an affirmative solution to both concerns…

Subliminal affirmations software

Leading up to that solution, let me just say that should you wish to broaden out your agenda to using affirmations, then a quick search on the Web will produce a number of websites, and YouTube videos, offering affirmations most probably appropriate to your needs.

But you could take using affirmations to a different level. You can do this by using subliminal affirmation software on your computer or tablet. Using such software will firstly require zero effort on your part for an affirmation to be said, displayed, and repeated.

And secondly, not having involvement with having to focus on and say the affirmation, it can more readily bypass the filter of the conscious mind and hit home to the subconscious – which, in my opinion, makes the procedure a lot more powerful.

Programs, such as Subliminal Power, Brain Bullet and Mindzoom, provide subliminal affirmations set to flash up on your screen every so many seconds, in a regulated fashion – for as long as you want them to.

It is usual to set for many hundreds being flashed up in any given hour. The idea is that, while you are busy on your computer the software is running, displaying affirmations that are too quick to consciously register but are picked up by your subconscious mind, and acted upon.

In using such software, you are usually able to select from "out of the box" affirmations (that you can also edit and add to), linked to a range of popular categories. My personal favourite program is Mindzoom.[2] With this you can also write your own affirmations – and even set them to subliminal audio with music.

References

1. Visit https://someinspiration.com/changeyourlife/selfhypnosis/self-hypnosis-downloads/ to find out more about Hypnosis Downloads.
2. Visit https://someinspiration.com/shop/mindzoom-your-way-to-success/ to find out more about MindZoom.

Steps to Using Creative Visualisation Part 1

While you are looking to making improvements at the level of your subconscious mind, let me ask you; how often have you heard someone say, "Come on, use your imagination?"

It is usually said in some kind of challenging or derogatory manner but actually, from another angle, it is not a bad suggestion. Your imagination is more powerful than you might think. I'm talking about using your imagination in context with *creative visualisation.*

In part one of this two-part item, I want to briefly cover how I learnt about creative visualisation, plus give an example of my experience of it. In the second part I'll be covering the steps you need to take to apply it in your life.

Creative visualization is the dynamic process of using the mind to create mental images of what one wants to have happen, or attract into one's life.

Creative visualisation in healing

The actual term itself I first came across back in the late 1970s. This was in context with the healer, Matthew Manning.

Manning was helping people heal themselves through his "Fighting Back" series of visualisation recordings. He was helping people to fight all kinds of medical problems using this technique. I got involved and for a while I helped him to distribute his programs through my contacts, and at a few holistic health exhibitions I did with him around London.

In order for his technique to work, he encouraged the vision, the client was to hold onto, to be of their own creation, to be powerful and uncompromising.

If you had a cancer for example you might conjure up your immune system as a powerful army that is then mobilised to blitz the cancerous cells. Or with, say, varicose veins possibly visualise a fish travelling through, unblocking and cleansing the veins.

The recommended visualisation procedure would be done three or four times a day until the target condition was eradicated.

This procedure could readily be used alongside orthodox medical practice/support or medication the sufferer might also be using. Using visualisation can only help whatever else one is doing or taking. Indeed one could so easily use visualisation in context with any medication doing its job.

This certainly was a complementary medicine that, according to Manning, worked well for a great number of people.

Creative visualisation and Technologies for Creating

Some years later, in the mid-1980s, I attended a course in creative visualisation with an organisation called, *Technologies for Creating* (TFC). This was setup by Robert Fritz (author of *The Path of Least Resistance*). I did the course, in London, and a further course to become a TFC practitioner.

TFC training essentially helps the learner to use creative visualisation for whatever they so desire – within ethical guidelines of course. I so recall how exciting it all was, from the bat, and how things really did happen as wished for. I got really sold on the idea then and I continue to explore and use the technique today.

Creative visualisation – a personal example

My first experience of using creative visualisation took place years before I met Matthew Manning and did the TFC training. This was when I was in my mid-twenties. Back then, I hadn't even heard of the term. It was this experience that also sparked my wanting to explore what magic lay behind what I went through – to find out how it worked.

At the time I was conjuring up, in my mind's eye, a vocation that entailed working in a modern building on some kind of investigative work. This was in a location that had open parkland, trees and water – involving a river and lakes. It was an idyllic quiet location, spacious, and suited my desire to be doing something that involved research. Research into what though, I had no idea at the time.

I'll call what I was doing "daydreaming" for want of a better word. On this basis I'd have to describe it as a recurring daydream. I had a snapshot in my mind of this scenario, that I dwelt on as something I would like to have happen. I often visited it, but not with any kind of planned regularity, any technique or clear intention.

My daydream was usually sparked by a book I might be reading, or by taking a walk in the countryside – something that inspired me and got me thinking. These activities definitely helped to drive my imagination and to retain the vision I had.

Workwise, I was then a sheet-metal worker, working for a small company on an industrial park in Leicestershire. Before that I had worked in a woodworking job. I was still living at my parents' home. I had no academic qualifications to speak of back then – I pursued much of my formal education some years later.

I'm telling you this because I want you to see that in contrast with the content of my vision, the possibility of any of it becoming real was pretty unlikely, arguably little more than a passing fantasy. But that didn't stop me from seeing it or indeed wishing I could live in it.

Three years on in this story and my secure sheet-metal job came to a rather abrupt end. This was following a workers strike. It resulted in a number of staff losing their jobs – myself included. It transpired to be a turning point for me. It was a changeful and scary time.

I applied for other sheet-metalwork jobs, attended interviews, and got offered work, but I wasn't entirely at ease taking up any of the posts offered. I was going through a change of heart. I began to see my "out of work" dilemma as an opportunity to go in a new direction.

A bit of synchronicity...

After a few months, in this unresolved situation, an interesting ("remarkable" to my mind) bit of synchronicity happened... I was in a bar, in Leicester, sharing a drink with a close friend (John Lucas). We talked about my situation, and how I had decided to get into some kind of community work or service. I mentioned that archaeology was on my mind, but that it seemed a long shot option...

As it happened we arranged to meet up again the next day. When we met it soon became obvious, from John's beaming face, that he had something interesting to discuss with me. "Here," he said, "take a look at this." He handed me the local, Leicester Mercury, evening newspaper. There on the front page was an item about current archaeology in Leicester with comments by local archaeologist, Jean Mellor.

The item though contained more than just an update on the finds that were being made; Mellor was actually making a plea, through the paper, for volunteers. She was seeking people to come along and help finish an important Roman rescue excavation in St Nicholas Circle in the town – before the "bulldozers moved in."

Well, how spooky was that? I couldn't help but smile at John. What a surprise! Talk about timing. I hardly ever bought this paper, and, apart from the timing of it, had John not bought it, and then let me know about it, well I may never have found out about the opportunity.

This was a big green light for my new direction if ever there was one. So, the next day I went along and joined the excavation team – simple as that. Thus began what was to become career, spanning a decade, in rescue archaeology.

I might add that months after my starting John also got involved in archaeology. Indeed, he later became the curator at Leicester's Jewry Wall Museum.

Away from Leicester, I worked as a volunteer on a lot of sites in different parts of the UK, notably in the Midlands, Yorkshire and Dorset; on sites ranging from Neolithic to Mediaeval. This also included working at Peterborough in Cambridgeshire. After about three years of moving around I was offered an opportunity to return to Peterborough to take up a permanent supervisory post.

The city was being developed as a "new town" at the time and rescue archaeology played an important role in its development. Not surprising really as Peterborough is built on the Anglo-Saxon town of Medeshamstede, while the Roman (pottery making) township, of Durobrivae, also lies on its borders.

Now before I continue, let me return to comment on my vision of the life I envisaged: Following my entry into archaeology my vision had been left somewhat on the back burner. I hadn't forgotten about it, rather I was having too many adventures to think that much about it. But that was about to change...

Suddenly it all fell into place...

Going with the Peterborough post was the opportunity to live in a recently converted flat, within an older, possibly 1930s house (called Ham Lane House), that was out in the sticks. It's the same house that I also mention in my book, *Life and Death: Making Sense of It*, for other reasons. The rest of the house had been converted into offices. A purpose-built lab and storage area had also been built onto one side of the house, to turn the whole structure into an archaeological field centre.

The building stood alone within surrounding fields – some of which were soon to become part of a golf course. The Nene Valley (steam) Railway ran (still does) close by. Much of the surrounding land was being quarried for gravel at the time I moved in, and much of the area looked like an industrial wasteland; "a bit bleak" would be a fair description. Amey Roadstone (construction company), were a year or so away from finishing up.

I then discovered, by talking with them, that the broader site was to be developed into parkland. Large areas of the gravel excavations were being turned into lakes. There was a nearby river, the River Nene, running past the development.

Suddenly, the penny dropped; it all fell into place. Here I was working and living in a modern building (part modern at least, and certainly for modern usage), in a location that had open parkland, and water, involving a river and lakes. I was doing research too. I was even employed by an organisation having "Research" in its title, the Nene Valley Research Committee. My daydream had become a reality – wow!

With my work, I lived in that romantic location for another six years before moving on – to further my education as it happens. By then it had become well established as Ferry Meadows (to me) or Nene Park[1] as it is now called – a great place to visit if you are in the Peterborough area.

This stuff really works...

Creative visualisation definitely does work. It works through the much popularised Law of Attraction. One uses the power of the mind to change something or to bring something towards one.

As I hope I'm managing to get across, it also has kinship with the use of hypnosis – which, I would recommend you use in tandem to get the best from both.

An art to be mastered

It needs be borne in mind that creative visualisation is an art-form, a skill to learn and master. The holistic theory behind it is generally well-received. Visualising outcomes is well-known to be used in sport for example, particularly in athletics and swimming.

The practice is another matter. You will get better at it the more you practice and get the technique right. Each person is also different in the way they work with it. This is simply because each of us is unique – and how we interact with the Law of Attraction is unique to our situation, and our energy.

What we can attract hinges on *resonance*. Bear this in mind as you read through the following, Steps to Using Creative Visualisation, Part 2. I will be saying more on it shortly.

References

1. Go to https://www.nenepark.org.uk/ to find out more about Nene Park.

Steps to Using Creative Visualisation Part 2

Putting creative visualisation into practice

The following steps offer you the foundation to begin creating what you want from life. But, you know the story – *be careful what you wish for*.

The steps to consider, in brief:

Step 1. Draw up a list
Step 2. Go for what you really want
Step 3. Goals achievable and recognisable
Step 4. A time frame may be desirable
Step 5. Read your list
Step 6. Visualise
Step 7. Current Reality
Step 8. Take action
Step 9. Believe, receive and be grateful
Step 10. Make a vision board (optional)

Step 1. Draw up a list

On proviso you have taken note of the comments in Part 1; draw up a list of what you want to have happen. Ask yourself what it is you really want or need, and build it from there.

Write your choices in the present tense as if it has already happened – even where you are placing a desire in a time frame, make it in the present when you come to visualise it.

Hone your list: I suggest you don't make your list too long. Consider keeping it to five or six choices, at least to begin with. Keep it simple and clear.

Begin each item with, "I choose …"

I suggest you also have a "quick-win" in your list. This is something that shouldn't take too long to manifest, something that you want to go well.

It could be as simple as signs of an improving relationship with a neighbour, losing a couple of pounds in weight, getting some good news about a project at work, or even someone special offering to buy you a cup of coffee today.

A quick-win will help to give you feedback and confidence in making this work. Hone your list until you get it right.

Step 2. Go for what you really want

Remember, creative visualisation works best when you, and what you desire, are realistic and in harmony with your own (inner) nature. **It needs to feel right, feel good**.

The choices you are making need to be something you really want to have happen. Avoid going down the route of choosing something fanciful that you wouldn't really accept if the opportunity arose.

Get in touch with your heart of hearts on this. I would suggest from the get-go you endeavour to dig behind each choice you are making, to find if there could be another bigger choice, or need, lurking.

Do also consider including fundamental choices in your listing, around your health and well-being. For example, you may choose along the lines of being:

- o healthy/having vitality
- o the predominant creative force in your life
- o honest and true to yourself
- o free to be yourself, having the freedom to choose

You can make choices regarding something you want to achieve for another person, perhaps a gift or a surprise. But avoid making choices on their behalf – it must come from them, their own will. That said, visualising in tandem on shared goals, however, can be a powerful way of working – doubling up on the power of intention.

Step 3. Select goals achievable and recognisable

The outcomes you are choosing need to be both achievable and recognisable when you receive them. In other words, you need to be able to gauge an outcome, to say it has happened, is complete.

So, needing a new car is an objective and easy to recognise when it arrives. It is easier than say, wanting a "better life" or "more money." These are too general to be easily recognised.

If it is a better life, then define what this means for you and break it into something achievable and recognisable in your vision. If it's money you want then state the amount clearly in your vision.

But also recognise where you may be making choices that are essentially a part of the process of getting from A to B – with B being the end goal you have in mind. If the money is for a car – then visualise the car, not the money.

Step 4. A time frame may be desirable

A time frame is sometimes desirable for when you want things to happen by. But by the same token there is no fixed time limit for a given outcome – it will depend upon you.

If you want something to arrive by a certain day or month, imagine being at that day or month, and receiving what you have chosen. How does it feel now the moment has arrived?

If something you want hasn't manifested by a certain time, try to understand why, rather than give up on it. Reconsider the steps above. Look at it from a different perspective. Very possibly there is something else that needs to happen first, or is blocking its arrival. Modify your choices where needed.

Step 5. Read your list

Read your list, out loud where/when possible. It is recommended you do it three times a day, morning, noon and night-time. Try it out for size and adjust your practice accordingly.

Try to make it feel fresh and alive each time you do it – avoid turning it into a chore or a habit. This can be difficult to get right. Perhaps you could read your list with accompanying uplifting, inspiring music; and use different tracks to keep things fresh. Importantly though, update your list, and rewrite it daily if need be. Keep it as a work in progress.

Step 6. Visualise

I suggest, in context with seeking your inner state of harmony, that you visualise one key item on your list rather than try to visualise them all. A visual snapshot of each and a fuller visualisation on one item is an alternative.

Visualising is THE hugely important step in this whole procedure. Some people believe they are unable to visualise. I'd say we are all capable of visualising and it will come with practice if you find it difficult to start with.

We mostly visualise on auto-pilot. For instance a family member phones us and we'll instantly have a picture in our mind of what that person looks like. It probably will not be in sharp relief, in part because we are not consciously focussed on conjuring an image of someone we know so well – we don't need to – but it will be there.

If you experience difficulty visualising, try starting with a simple object. For example visualise a tree right now... I'll bet a tree popped into your mind. I've got a beautifully formed tree, with all its leaves in full bloom. If you are not certain you have a tree then get a pencil and a piece of paper, and draw the tree you are seeing. Make it as close as possible. Try seeing your tree at a different time of year.

Try to visualise another object and draw it. Given you are not in Cairo right now, try visualising one and draw that, now do the three major Egyptian pyramids and draw these; perhaps with a camel beside them for good measure.

Really get into it

Visualise what you want. When visualising really get into it. Let your imagination run riot but also keep your feet on the ground. You want that house or flat – then go inside the place, in your head. You are working with the ideal and bringing it into manifestation.

Check out what you want the rooms to look like, what the garden (if it has one) looks like. Picture yourself doing a tour around it. Consider even using props to help you. What is really important is to get into what you are after so that it is already real and you are "living it" – and living it now.

You want to be wealthy then try wearing your best clothes and go out, or even around your home, in style. Get into the feeling of being the person you want to be.

What can be really powerful is to weave your choices together into a mental script for a story or play that resolves in the best outcome. Make yourself the main character and routinely live it as if it is already happening – until it does.

A word of caution

Having suggested pinning things down in detail there are instances where it may be preferable to allow things to remain a bit fuzzy.

Let's say, for example, you are seeking a beautiful spot to live in and have your mind set on a particular location, house and garden design. It stands to reason that, unless you have already seen the house, garden and location you want (and are waiting for it to come onto the market – like Agatha Christie did with her beloved "Greenway" in Devon), the ideal which you are rooting for may not indeed exist.

Also, if you are working with a partner on this then there is more room for differences in what you are both seeking. Being overly specific may turn out not to be what you both want or need. In context, have a look at Step 10.

It's a balancing act where combinations of desires are involved – and pretty surely there may be one or two compromises to make.

Step 7. Current Reality

While visualising, keep in touch with your "current reality" – where you are now, in contrast to where you want to be. Robert Fritz (mentioned in Part 1) considers that this creates a dynamic tension (like a stretched rubber band) that will help propel you towards your goal. It is a means of gauging how things are developing.

In your visualising, work with current reality by shifting focus between where you are, or what you have now; and what you want, or where you want to be.

Step 8. Take action

Another important step. Using visualisation you are working with the Law of Attraction. You are saying to the cosmic mind (or whatever you wish to call it, or view it; for some of us it is the subconscious mind, and both), this is what I want. There is (in theory) no need to be concerned with how this "want" is going to appear, rather you trust that it will. It helps to retain a light-heartedness about it too – more on this below.

Events can move in mysterious ways when you are working dynamically with thought. Things can happen as if by magic. Synchronistic events can happen "out of the blue" so to speak, unexpected and seemingly unconnected with what is desired. This has everything to do with resonance – building resonance is key. Things can seemingly fall into your lap when in the zone of the right moment and the right frame of mind.

Even so you are advised to also use common sense and be proactive to help bring about what you want where you can.

It does depend upon what you are seeking but consider, for instance, would this book have appeared if I hadn't acted upon the vision of it? Ideas usually need a helping hand to be brought into reality. Recognise and act on opportunity as it arises.

Go with what you feel to be right while keeping your focus on objectives, end results. Take advantage of opportunity that may come your way, to help you get to where you truly want to be. You may well need your wits about you at times too. Sure, you'll probably make mistakes but you are learning your art.

Step 9. Believe, receive and be grateful

Some will say it is not essential to believe that creative visualisation will produce results, in order so as to manifest results. The results will come if you keep your focus on what it is that you want.

I can see that this can work. When I was seeing being involved in, "investigative work ... in open parkland ... involving a river and lakes," I didn't consider whether I believed this could come about or not – indeed I didn't give it that much thought either way. I wasn't expecting it to happen or that it was possible for it to happen. It was more like a vision I escaped into, wishing it would happen.

Later I came to realise, notably through Matthew Manning's work, that having belief and expectation is essential to bring about results.

It is important to believe in the procedure and to expect results. If you are going to use this procedure to help cure cancer, for example, you will need a powerful "forces mobilised" vision that is backed up with the expectation of successful outcomes.

So in context, *believe* in receiving what you want. And as you actually receive an outcome, fully receive it. And be thankful, be grateful. Indeed make gratitude a part of your daily process.

Take the item off your list. Review your list once more.

Note, in terms of reviewing your list, things can also change whereby a choice you are making today you will want to discard tomorrow – as it no longer appeals or applies – and that is par for the course.

Step 10. Make a vision board (optional)

A great way to help bring about the results you want is by creating a vision board that incorporates your goals.

This can include anything – pictures, items, quotes, drawings, plans, mind maps, etc. – placed on a large sheet of paper, on a wall or fridge or home notice board. A cork board, that you can easily pin items onto, is a good idea. I suggest you make it colourful, fun and inspiring.

You can either let it happen by what "feels" right to place where, or organise into areas based upon what you desire.

There are a number of benefits to using a vision board. Some of the obvious ones are:

o You get to be reminded of your goals each time you look at it – even subconsciously glancing at it.
o It supports visualising – as it can provide a half-way house of bringing things closer to reality than a simple text list.
o It allows you to stand back and visually see how things can come together – and thereby make changes to your vision that could have a profound effect on outcomes.

Probably the most important benefit is as a necessary aid if you are visualising with a partner or group. A shared clear vision is powerful stuff.

Results

Results happen. They can happen quickly, or slowly, and in surprisingly unexpected and synchronistic ways. Results are dependent upon how well you can master and apply this art into your life.

Some of us grasp it quickly while some of us find it difficult. Some of us claim success at every turn, while others can vary where success is concerned.

Obstacles to success

One of the main obstacles on the road of being successful with creative visualisation will be yourself – indeed I'd go so far as to say it is the only real obstacle.

A lot of the reason why this approach may not work for a person will be due to their subconscious narrative that invokes an, "I can't" do this or achieve that, or "I don't believe" this or that is possible, or "I don't deserve" this or that into my life.

This can be deep rooted, from years (especially growing years, as discussed earlier) of experience.

A point I make in the book, *Life and Death: Making Sense of It,* is that we have all learnt from an early age to be cautious in what we believe. This is not a bad thing per se as we have to negotiate a world that is not all that it seems. And it can be damaging too...

Do you recall how you were once led to believe in Father Christmas? Do you recall how you later discovered that you had been duped into believing in this magical being. Do you recall who had duped you into believing it? Most probably it was by, of all people, your parent/s.

Possibly you do not remember what it was like when finding out such a being didn't exist but the experience, the disappointment, and possibly embarrassment, went into your young mind, as indeed it did for probably most of us reading this.

I'm not suggesting that we stop children from believing in Father Christmas. These days it is an intrinsic part of children's initiation across much of the globe. But I am saying that such an initiation can have a profound impact on how open or closed our minds are to possibilities in later life – and it might help if we don't use it to quash a child's belief in possibilities that we think are impossible.

With a mindset predisposed to disbelief (we don't get fooled again) it becomes easier for us to doubt anything sounding magical, like creative visualisation or the Law of Attraction, than to embrace it, and the powerful concepts associated with it.

With this we are back to considering our subconscious mind. Our subconscious mind, by what it has been taught, can sabotage our (new) belief in what is and isn't possible in other words. This is obviously where, again, hypnosis can come into its own to help to change this.

Another important factor to consider, in our success with bringing about the outcomes we want, is *timing*. Few experts on the Law of Attraction ever talk about this important component.

Firstly I've noted there is a kind of "beginner's luck" in how this law operates. It seems to work best at the point of initiation when there is a lot of good intention, innocence and hope around. After that the effects can drop off.

This does give a clue to the need to retain the excitement of beginning something new and to remain optimistic and light-footed about it. The trick is to play with it and not let things get too routine, too involved or too serious. **Being creative is to play**.

Secondly we live in a dynamic changing and, I would say, *meaningful* world – with a great many moving parts, that include ourselves. What opportunity is there right now, today, will not be quite the same tomorrow – it could be better, it could be more challenging. At times our lives more easily resonate with the flow of things, and everything can seem easy-peasy. At other times we are challenged and may have to stretch ourselves that extra mile to bring about anything like the end result we desired. We are all learners in the art of living in this new dynamic world that we are slowly waking up to.

Remember then that patience is a virtue and how important it is to consciously lift our resonance with the world around us to be successful.

Improve your resonance for good things to happen

I want to make a really important point here as to why most of us get this whole thing wrong. And I've left it to last to allow you to be able to gauge if you (in working back through the steps above) are making the same mistake as most of us.

When working with creative visualisation, and The Law of Attraction, we will tend to think of all the experiences and things we want to have, to improve our lives; and as a result we tend to place the focus "out there," on those objective experiences or things to come into our lives, to make us happy.

We need to consider that one's focus, instead, needs to start with the "inner" rather than the "outer." This is a principle that Charles Haanel stresses in his, *The Master Key System*, and is also endorsed in the Eastern approach to karma. There is a subtle but crucial difference in the orientation of how one then goes about working with visualisation.

The ongoing situation that you or I are in at the present time, whether we are happy in it or not, is the result of our past attitude and beliefs. This is what we have brought ourselves to. We have created it – most probably unconsciously. So in order to bring about the change/s we so desire in our outer circumstances now, we must first be those changes within ourselves. We adjust our inner life so that the desired external change/s can follow.

It is not enough that we focus on what we want from out there; where we make our wishes and it magically manifests into our lives regardless of where we are at in ourselves. Don't hold your breath for it to arrive on that basis – it most probably won't. This is the impression one might, for example, have taken away from watching the film, *The Secret*. It appears to be all easy-peasy.

When I review how it has happened in my life, it is following a change in myself, a change in my buoyancy, a change of heart, a change of direction, a change in expectation. Or possibly even a "nudge" to move in a certain direction. But it is not by the mere wanting something to occur.

This is a matter of focus, we change our self, we live with love, humility, discipline, authenticity and integrity, and what we desire, in context, will then tend to follow naturally.

So, you create an inner vision. Make it an inner vision that includes peace, harmony and balance, an inner vision of happiness and abundance, an inner vision of success.

If you get this right, and work with it, what can then happen is that the external world will begin to change to meet and mirror your internal vision. The things you desire will come towards you through this resonance, rather than any abracadabra conscious choices or manipulation.

You need to get this... This is part of the art I was talking about. It presents us with a much bigger perspective on how it all works – and possibly what higher understanding we may be getting into by pursuing it.

> What you are, is what you have been, what you will become, is what you do now.
>
> Gautama Buddha

To improve your resonance, for what you want, practice keeping your thoughts and inner vision on an even and positive keel. This will take effort. No doubt about it...

Notice your thoughts, and how you verbalise your thoughts, as you go through your day. Just be aware and pick yourself up if you are tending to be negative with yourself, your situation, and/or with others – and change the record. Use whatever means or technique you have at your disposal (apply the advice listed in this book) to regroup, and keep up good, uplifting and proactively happy thoughts throughout your day. This helps to remove blocks and generate resonance with what you are seeking.

Armed with these thoughts on developing an "inner vision" which results in a change in your resonance, go back over the steps you have taken above to see where you can, or need, to revise your approach, and make appropriate adjustments.

Consider writing a script, a narrative to the things you want, instead of a simple check list. See it all as a work in progress, an art to be developed with practice, to make perfect.

And check out the following Body and Spirit sections to help you on your journey to a successful life...

A couple of good books

In context with the above, here's a reminder to consider getting hold of a copy of *The Master Key System* by Charles F Haanel (visit SomeInspiration.com and look under Books menu). This book offers a 24-part course in getting visualisation right, and getting this approach to life nailed. It is a very special book.

I'd also recommend you read Lynn Grabhorn's book, *Excuse Me, Your Life is Waiting*. My editor put me onto it and it is not only a great read but also a good reference work in support of living successfully, with the Law of Attraction.

Body

Simple Steps to help get your body into gear

There is a vast amount of information and advice available to read in newspapers, on television, and on the web these days about health and exercise. It can get very confusing to know what is best, so I've stuck with some basics here, and making salient points which align with the thoughts and practices in the rest of this book.

Simple Steps to Get Healthy and Stay Healthy

As we say, *prevention is better than cure*, and making a few adjustments in the way we live will help us to prolong our health, avoid getting ill or coming to rely heavily on medical fixes.

Here are some "down-home" steps for staying young and healthy – to help you maintain a long and healthy life:

Step 1. Get Enough Exercise
Step 2. Sleep when you're sleepy
Step 3. Wash with cool water
Step 4. Get up early every day
Step 5. Eat when you feel hungry
Step 6. Give your digestive system a holiday
Step 7. All work no play... Well!

You will find in addition that these steps can help you to lose weight if you need to.

Step 1. Get Enough Exercise

What I'm going to say here isn't aimed at the person who is training for a marathon or triathlon right now, but at those of us who may be starting from the couch-potato position, where physical activity is somewhere towards the bottom of our daily agenda, or list of things to do.

Photo: Daniela Corno

I'd encourage you to get yourself out, right now, and go for a 20 minute walk – or cycle ride or a swim. Do some physical activity daily. Walking, cycling or swimming is great for the body and overall good health. It reduces stress and helps us to relax better.

Of course these days, it goes without saying, we have come to rely less on our bodies for getting around and to rely more on other forms of transport – especially our cars.

Years ago people relied less on cars and walked or cycled to their nearest shop, school, or place of work. Back then probably there was also more physical movement at one's place of work, than there is now. Today so many of us can spend our working time sitting down, with our fingers doing all the walking.

Physical inactivity, as we're beginning to realise all too well, is one of the main reasons for a host of concerns and diseases. We need to add some form of exercise into our daily routine, particularly if our normal day does not require that much physical exertion.

Walk to somewhere inspiring, uplifting

When taking a walk for health, if you are in a position to, target some inspiring countryside or location – choose the best spots. And get away from traffic.

Some years back I lived in London's East End and I was a bit short on inspiring scenery. If I took a walk, or a run, I usually plotted in visiting a park, a few blocks away, and especially past a local library fairly close by. The library had some beautiful maple trees outside of it. Believe it or not I could feel better, uplifted, for incorporating that bit of nature into my route.

Take it gently

If you haven't exercised for a long time you will need to take things gently and build up - don't do too much too soon; pace it!

It is not necessary for exercise to be that strenuous either but it does help to have at least one exercise in your toolbox that causes you to pant a bit – like running on the spot, squats or push-ups which are good cardio-vascular exercises. These exercises also help build muscle too; to better aid our coping with everyday tasks.

Moderate exercise, that includes walking, cycling or swimming as the prime component, will be an effective way to get started on regular exercising. This is especially so if you need to lower your blood pressure, and definitely if you're just beginning on a fitness programme.

A suggested starter programme for walking

If starting from scratch look to getting a routine together - that you toughen up and develop as you get stronger. Be disciplined about it. You might like to try this:

- o Week 1: Walk for 20 minutes every other day – 10 minutes to the turning point, or use a circular route. Rest on in-between days.
- o Week 2 to 4: Walk for 20 minutes on four days. On the fifth day take a 30 minute walk. Rest for two days. Decide how best to divide up the week between walking and resting.
- o Week 5 to 8: Walk for 30 minutes on most days.
- o Week 9 onwards: Walk for 30 minutes on most days. Take an hour walk (3 to 4 miles round trip) on one day a week.

Soon you'll be on your way to getting your own regular routine going – and feeling better for it. Keep it up. Bear in mind that, given the "bug bites," you could actually walk a marathon if you so wished. You are not obligated to run it in other words. Check out **The Walking Site**[1] for additional help.

Some ifs:

- o If you have a medical condition it will be wise to check with your doctor for their advice first – before starting an exercise routine of any nature.

- If you are somehow stuck in your home, or with limited mobility, take a look on the Web for exercises you might use to keep yourself fit. For example check out **HelpGuide**[2] or **Disabled World**.[3] Broadly, regular physical movement of any form is going to help.
- If you spend a lot of time sitting down, because of your work, then get up, stretch and take a short walk – around your swivel chair at very least. Do the routine at least every hour. It'll probably also give your eyes a bit of a break too.

  In any case, if working at a computer, it is required health and safety practice to rest your eyes for 5 to 10 minutes in every hour. This way you can combine it with a stretch and short walk exercise.

Exercise in the home might involve:

- Gentle stretching (incorporating touching your toes or endeavouring to) for 3 repetitions.
- Getting up and down steps until you are panting a bit – try (or build up to) 10 repetitions up and down your stairs.
- Sitting down and getting up again, first off a kitchen chair and later doing the same off an armchair for 3 repetitions.
- Doing squats – try building up to 10 repetitions.

This is all good for building leg muscle and helping you to get, and keep fit.

Get the balance right

Exercise such as walking and stretching can be done daily. If you decide to embark on more strenuous exercise, in a gym or at home, such as press-ups and using weights, consider doing so for around 30 minutes each session, and then for three or four times a week – with rest days in

between.

The more strenuous the exercise you do, the more you will be breaking down muscle tissue, and correspondingly will need rest days for your body to recover, repair and get stronger. I have exercised all my life and I know first-hand how important it is to rest the body between exercising to achieve a proper balance, and especially as one gets older.

By the way you can expect to ache a bit with the muscles you are exercising. This is quite normal, particularly if you haven't exercised in years, or are trying something requiring more energy and effort.

Step 2. Sleep when you're sleepy

This may sound self-evident but a great many of us do have a tendency to stay up late even when our body is telling us that it is time to sleep.

Sleep experts remind us that our natural rhythm is to sleep in the night and be active during the day – sounds obvious. However quite a lot of us choose to stay up late into the night.

Some people because of their work, of course, have less choice in the matter. Others do have a choice but instead have got into the habit of remaining active at night and sleeping well into the day – or not so well and getting only a few hours' refreshing sleep.

While we can do this for a time, the argument is that it will eventually take a toll on our health. Complementary health practitioners say that this kind of unnatural living is one of the contributing factors in the causation of cancer and other diseases.

The body needs good sleep to rest and repair itself.

You also need to rest in a restful environment. Your bedroom needs to be for sleeping. I suggest you remove all clutter, newspapers, magazines and any electronic equipment from your bedroom – get that TV and tablet out of there. It needs to be balanced, peaceful and harmonious – to recharge your batteries not the batteries of your electronic equipment.

Try catnapping

If you are suffering from a shortage of sleep-time and are able to catnap (or power nap), then do so. This is one sure way of refreshing your system and helping you to be more alert and energised. It shouldn't of course be an alternative to regular sleep at a regular time.

Catnaps can be anywhere between a few minutes to an hour. Twenty minutes is a good rule of thumb. I've found fifteen to twenty minutes is about right for me. This holds me at a hypnagogic level or shallow sleep.

Going over this can take me into a deeper sleep and then leave me feeling drowsy rather than refreshed when I awake. It is interesting to note that (like discussed in the hypnosis topic) if you do this on a regular basis, your body will instinctively know when time is up – otherwise you may have to set a timer.

Tip: If you really want to buzz on awaking, try having a cup of coffee before your catnap. It'll kick-in as you awake 20 minutes later.

Step 3. Wash with cool water before going to bed

Brrr – okay, sounds simple enough...

After a long day wash with cool – rather than hot – water in the shower or bath. It might surprise you but the cool water will help to reduce your stress levels, and thereby help you to relax. It will prepare you for a deep refreshing sleep.

Try it, it does work. This is also why swimming in cool water can be so good at helping us to become invigorated, to relax and to sleep better at night. Other benefits are said to include improvement of our skin, hair, our immune system, and to encourage weight loss.

Step 4. Get up early every day

Following on from getting regular sleep, the old proverb, *Early to bed, early to rise makes a person healthy, wealthy and wise*, is appropriate here.

It may not bring you wealth by itself but it will certainly help you to stay healthy. Your body needs just enough sleep, not too much and not too little – around 7 to 8 hours is the general advice but can vary from person to person.

Step 5. Eat when you feel hungry

Now this is a tough one to get to grips with because most of us have learnt to eat at set times and we will tend to eat at those times – and in between if not careful; and regardless of whether we really need to or not.

It is actually better for us to eat when we are hungry (taking small portions) as the danger is that we will not digest our food properly if we eat it when we don't need it. Acidity and indigestion can begin, and this contributes to the likelihood of other more complex health issues taking root.

And eat well...

If you live in the UK, you'll probably know this NHS advice:

- o Eat at least 5 portions of a variety of fruit and vegetables every day.
- o Base your meals on higher fibre starchy foods like potatoes, bread, rice or pasta.
- o Bran flakes and muesli with grapes has to be one of my favourite breakfast meals. Of course you need to have some milk or dairy alternatives (such as soya milk) with that.
- o Eat some beans, pulses, fish, white meats and other protein.
- o Choose unsaturated oils and spreads.
- o And drink plenty of fluids – the recommendation is 6 to 8 glasses a day.

Step 6. Give your digestive system a holiday

Another toughie… Unless you have been advised otherwise, by your doctor, it is good to give your digestive system a rest periodically.

Eat less for a day each month

Consider refraining from eating anything altogether for one complete day a month. Alternatively only eat a small amount of raw food, such as fruit, for one complete day a month. Drink only water on that day. This procedure both gives your digestive organs a rest and also helps in the elimination of waste from your body.

If you eat meat on a regular basis I'd further recommend you go vegetarian for at least one day a week. This can only help your system keep in check the potential toxins in meat products.

Opportune lifestyle moment

Here's a suggestion: Combine the practice of giving your system a rest, or a change, with dipping into an inspirational book, relaxing music (maybe relaxation music like my partner **Annie Locke**[4] produces), or follow a spiritual pursuit for that day.

Heck, bear in mind that everything we take in is part of our diet. It is important to feed our mind and spirit, as our body.

And I would go further to suggest give up watching television, and, or not being online, for at least one day a month - and that could all be on the same "day of rest." Yes I know, the madness of such suggestions... But I dare you to try it and see the difference it makes.

Step 7. All work no play... Well!

Does it go without saying that we also need, for the best of health, to be on a diet of variety, the spice of life? I do hope so.

Sign up for a dose of adventure, laughter, song and dance, whatever hits the mark. Get outside of any routine that tends to close you down. Hugs are great too – try them, my partner swears by them.

Comment on further wholesome routines

I've kept the steps here simple and fundamental to improving all-round fitness and health, on an economical basis too. If you wished to take this a lot further I suggest you explore taking up yoga, tai-chi or a pilates class as a next step in your fitness campaign. These methods also help tie physical fitness in with the needs of your spirit.

Results

Follow these steps and you are on your way to a much healthier body. You'll feel better for it, feel lighter and more alive; and who knows what other benefits might creep in if you closely follow the simple practices outlined above. Happy living...

References

1. For The Walking Site go to http://thewalkingsite.com/
2. For HelpGuide.org exercises, go to https://www.helpguide.org/articles/healthy-living/chair-exercises-and-limited-mobility-fitness.htm
3. For Disabled World exercises go to https://www.disabled-world.com/fitness/exercise/
4. For Annie Locke's music visit https://annielocke.com

Spirit

Simple Steps to help you get in touch with your spirit

Whatever way you seek to improve the health of your mind and body, all improvement eventually amounts to nought unless placed in context with the needs and nourishment of your spirit.

Stepping The Eightfold Path

Siddhārtha Gautama, the Buddha, is attributed with originating the idea of liberation from the cycle of birth and death. He posited his plan of action in what he called, *The Eightfold Path* to freedom.

Now, you really don't have to be a Buddhist to see the sense and goodness of these eight pointers for how each of us should live on our beautiful planet. Okay some of the pointers might be in need of deeper study – such as understanding the Law of Karma – but let that be your next step. Practice this path, alongside the

Image: Jin Neoh

steps laid out elsewhere in this book and you should find peace in your heart and success in your life.

The Eightfold Path

1. Right view

Right view involves seeing things as they really are. That is, all things being in flux, in impermanence, and this in context with the Law of Karma.

If not clear, consider the Law of Karma as the much older name for the Law of Attraction and then, knowing that, see where that might take you in your understanding.

2. Right intention

Right intention involves the renunciation of desire. It involves embracing goodwill and kindness towards all beings.

Treat all beings with goodwill and kindness, and all involvement in the world in moderation. If you consider that our ultimate goal is to remove ourselves from the lower vibration of physical existence then the comment about "desire" will make sense – even if very challenging for many of us to put into practice.

3. Right speech

Right speech invokes moral discipline, ethical conduct, being honest and straight with others – as indeed ourselves. It also requires we bring no harm to others through what we say privately or publicly.

4. Right action

Right action invokes healthy and proper conduct in one's activities – and avoiding actions that can harm others or oneself.

5. Right livelihood

Right livelihood requires us to acquire an honest and healthy means of making a living, and living within our means. It is based upon harmlessness towards all beings.

6. Right effort

Right effort requires one's efforts being placed in a wholesome direction, supporting the mind – and moving away from misdirected effort that is harmful to others or oneself.

7. Right mindfulness

Right mindfulness invokes being mindful, taking charge of our thinking, our thoughts, and directing them towards wholesome ends.

8. Right concentration

Right concentration involves applying one's focus upon awakening, and lifting consciousness through meditation and contemplation.

Other comments by the Buddha

Work out your own salvation. Do not depend upon others. No one saves us but ourselves. No one can and no one may. We ourselves must walk the path.

There are only two mistakes one can make along the road to truth; not going all the way, and not starting.

Peace comes from within. Do not seek it without.

Results

Get this right and you are on your way to Nirvana. And you will be blessed for your efforts.

All in all, if you have worked through this book, and are incorporating all that it has to offer into your life, you will definitely be feeling the benefits in mind, body and spirit.

Steps to Meditation

I'm sure you know already that meditation is a great all-rounder for quietening the mind, lowering body stress levels, and bringing peace to one's life.

If not already using meditation to achieve such a desirable state, then the following steps will certainly help you to become familiar with it, and, in turn, help you to change how you perceive the world and yourself.

Photo: Tosaporn Boonyarangkul

During meditation the intention is to gently clear the mind of all noisy thoughts, and to achieve an inner stillness.

This is so easy a child could do it! Well, it might look easy but perhaps not so when getting down to doing it. One person may indeed find it relatively easy, while another find it tougher going. Generally our minds can be described as "busy" and difficult to quieten down – and there lies the work. Regardless, it is well-known that everyone can benefit from meditation with application and practice.

In Buddhism, meditation is treated as more than just a coping mechanism for life. It is used to gain clarity in understanding, lifting consciousness, and acknowledging that there are different levels to consciousness.

In other words, it is a means to familiarise oneself with one's truer nature. It is viewed as an essential method or way of preparing for life, death and enlightenment.

So now check out the following simple steps and tips to begin your meditation practice. Here they are in brief:

Step 1. Get in the right spot
Step 2. Remove constraints
Step 3. Get comfortable
Step 4. Switch on the Chi
Step 5. Stay awake
Step 6. Be mindful of your breath

Step 1. Get in the right spot

Find a quiet place where you will not be disturbed for 20 minutes or so each day.

If need be, lift the atmosphere of the room or location by keeping it tidy, peaceful, harmonious – remove any clutter and any electronic equipment where possible. If not already there, consider adding in a plant or two, such as the Peace Lily or French Lavender.

Step 2. Remove constraints

Remove or undo all clothing that constricts. Remove your watch for example. If you want to keep a check on the time, your watch could be useful to keep close by.

You want no tightness around your waist, or indeed any part of your body - so remove shoes, your tie, belt, and, or jewellery – anything that constricts.

Better still, start by wearing clothing that allows freedom of movement from the bat.

Also deal with any tightness or tension in your body - have a good stretch, tense and relax muscles, and wiggle your toes.

Photo: Chris Scott

Step 3. Get comfortable

Sit comfortably. If on a chair, use a dining chair or stool rather than an armchair. Keep your back straight - if the chair has a back avoid the temptation of leaning back against it.

There is no need to cross your legs, indeed, if you are using a chair, it will probably be more comfortable to have your feet firmly flat on the floor.

If you are more used to sitting in a lotus position then by all means do that, but it is not essential. Nor is it recommended if you have never sat in a lotus position before. There's no need to climb two mountains when one is enough for this purpose.

Step 4. Switch on the Chi

Rest your arms on your thighs with your palms turned upwards. Allow your index finger and thumb on each hand to be touching at the tips - imagine as you do this you are allowing the flow of chi energy through your body. It will have the effect of helping to centre you.

Some people find it helpful to touch the roof of the mouth with the tongue too – as this helps to complete a circuit and aids centring.

Step 5. Stay awake

Keep your eyelids open just a little - letting light in. This is a compromise: not having your eyes open helps you to avoid being distracted by anything around you in the room, whilst not being entirely closed helps to keep you present, awake. It is surprisingly easy to nod off when meditating with your eyes fully closed.

You may also find it helpful to focus your gaze on the space midway between your eyes. I've found this can be powerful and really helps one to be centred.

Also occasionally, just check your back is being kept straight, and make any adjustment necessary.

Step 6. Be mindful of your breath

Breathe normally and follow your breath. Listen in to your breath. As thoughts come up, and they will, gently steer yourself back to your breath.

You can chant the sacred sound "Om" to help keep your mind focused but if you feel a bit odd doing this then keep following your breath.

If you have hearing issues then focus on feeling the rise and fall of your breath.

That's it - that's all you need to do!

Is that really all one needs to do?

Well no. Let's talk practice and commitment!
You need to be able to commit to meditating once a day. To pursue this you need to be willing to do for 15 to 20 minutes - preferably first thing in the morning before taking breakfast.

With practice and development you may find it beneficial to extend this time gradually to twice as long – to 30 or 40 minutes a day. Some people choose to meditate twice a day, but I'd suggest you keep it simple, in keeping with developing a long-term practice – indeed develop your practice *organically* to suit your lifestyle.

Results

Results may happen quickly; but don't be surprised if you don't notice much change at the start.

After the initial enthusiasm to get your meditation practice under way it may even feel like a bit of a chore and an anti-climax for a while. However do keep at it and you will start to notice a sense of being more centred and at ease when you are meditating – and that sense can continue beyond your meditation and into your day.

This feeling will grow as you make meditation a part of your routine, a part of your life. It will calm you down and help you to achieve inner peace – a peace that starts to permeate through you and, if you let it, take over your life.

Desired goal

The desired goal of meditation is to be in a constant state of inner peace while about one's daily life and business. Now, that is some state to be in. And how wonderful will that be!?

A Loving Kindness Contemplation

Once you have begun to master meditation consider incorporating with it this "Loving Kindness" contemplation at the end of your session.

The suggestion is that you bring this into your meditation two or three times a week but by all means use every day if you so wish.

Image: by StockSnap from Pixabay

The practice for oneself

The practice involves firstly saying to yourself the words:

May I be well, happy, peaceful and calm. May I be protected from any harm. May I be well, happy, peaceful and calm.

If you wish, consider altering the wording to suit how you wish for the best for yourself today. It is easier to remember if you make any changes to rhyme.

Directing the practice towards others

Next, think of a person you love. Now also think of a person for whom you have no strong feelings. And then also think of a person who challenges you, or you have difficulty with, or cannot easily get on with.

And as you think of these people direct your words (those above) towards each in turn. Obviously change the "I" to "you" or preferably their name.

As you say the words visualise goodness flowing to the person you are contemplating.

Directing the practice towards the world

Next, you could end with the following for the world:

May all be well, peaceful and calm. May all be happy and protected from harm. May all be well, peaceful and calm.

Results

Don't be surprised if you receive unexpected benefits from your active words and thoughts – but likewise, don't look for such outcomes.

Try to see your activity as a service for the good of others – that they might receive benefits from your thoughts.

If you want to pursue this further, consider getting hold of the book, *Loving-Kindness Meditation* by Bill Scheffel.

Final comment

May you be well, happy, peaceful and calm. May you be protected from any harm.

And may this book become a useful *aide-memoire* to your journey of peace, worldly success and spiritual development.

Index

About The Author

Francis O'Neill writes about Mind, Body & Spirit, self-help, astrology and spiritual health matters.

Steps to Health, Wealth & Inner Peace, is his second book in the *Making Sense of It* series – from Some Inspiration Publications.

His earlier book, *Life and Death: Making Sense of It,* explores life in context with the afterlife through human evolution, consciousness, through the paranormal, through near-death experience, through past lives and reincarnation. With the aid of mediums and NDE reporting, it also pays a visit to the Other Side.

His third book is, *Love's Story of Why We Are Here.* This book seeks to answer one big question about life: **Why are we here?** It bridges the gap between the sciences and the spiritual. The author advances a revolutionary and exciting model of awakening/consciousness showing how everything has a role to play. This includes what he calls the *"soul ladder,"* an essential part of this model.

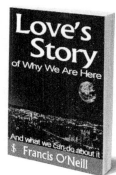

The author takes an investigative approach to mind, body & spirit matters. He has experienced, first-hand, something of the paranormal, and has spent over 40 years studying the spiritual and esoteric perspective on life. As well as being a professional astrologer and author, he has spent a good deal of his working life in archaeology and as a lecturer in adult education.

He lives in the Cotswolds (UK) with his partner, Annie Locke. Annie is better known for her relaxing and classical music (see AnnieLock.com). She is also the editor for his books. She used to be a script editor, so that helps.

You can find out more about the writer's books, and his interests, by visiting the publisher website, SomeInspiration.com.

Leave a review

If you have enjoyed reading this book, or found it helpful, please leave a review, on Amazon or wherever you got it from, so that others may also consider reading it. All reviews are greatly appreciated. Thank you in advance.

Printed in Great Britain
by Amazon